EBAY ARBITRAGE

5 STEPS TO MAKE RISK FREE MONEY WITHOUT INVESTMENT

By: Frank Knoll

TWK - Publishing

©2016

Copyright© 2016
TWK – Publications - twk-publishing.com - @Travis1177

All rights reserved. No part of this publication may be reproduced, distributed, or transmitted in any form or by any means, including photocopying, recording, or other electronic or mechanical methods, without the prior written permission of the publisher, except in the case of brief quotations embodied in critical reviews and certain other non-commercial uses permitted by copyright law.

While attempts have been made to verify that the information contained in this publication is accurate, neither the author nor the publisher assumes any responsibility for errors, omissions, interpretations or usage of the subject matters herein.

This publication contains the opinions and ideas of its author and is intended for informational purposes only. The author and publisher shall in no event be held liable for any loss or other damages incurred the usage of the publication.

Disclaimer

The information provided in this book is designed to provide helpful information on the subjects discussed. The publisher and author are not responsible for any specific health or allergy needs that may require medical supervision and are not liable for any damages or negative consequences from any treatment, action, application or preparation, to any person reading or following the information in this book. References are provided for informational purposes only and do not constitute endorsement of any websites or other sources. Readers should be aware that the website listed in this book may change.

Table of Contents

Introduction 1

Chapter 1 – Creating an eBay Seller Account 6

Chapter 2 – Finding Products to List 10

Chapter 3 – Listing Your Products... 16

Chapter 4 – Expand Your Service 26

Chapter 5 – Manage Your Business Through Outsourcing 31

Chapter 6 – Tim, the Online Store Expert................................. 34

Freedom: Your Ultimate Gain... 36

Introduction

Arbitrage. What does the term ring in your mind? I guess it will be a boring, financial and economic concept that has no relevance to you or should I say, you have no interest in understanding what arbitrage is.

Whatever be the case, you cannot escape arbitrage, and you will find this a widely used and accepted concept.

Before proceeding to define what arbitrage is or explaining how people utilize this, let me share an extremely simple example. This is something you may have observed and experienced in your day-to-day shopping.

Let's say you buy groceries from the local supermarket. Have you ever given a thought as to where the supermarket owner gets the groceries from? Let us become more specific now. Let's say you buy fruits and vegetables from the supermarket. Now, let me ask you the same question. Where does he get the green groceries from?

Think about your answer.

What answer did you think? Farmer? Wholesale market? Or did he grow his own fruits and vegetables?

If you thought the person grew his own fruits and vegetables, you are partially right because he can only sell so much with what he grows. Hence, he has to depend upon direct procurement from the farmer or purchase from the wholesale market.

When the supermarket guy purchases his grocery supplies from the farmer or the wholesale market, he buys at a low rate (because he buys in bulk) and sells the same goods at a higher rate in his supermarket.

The price difference between the buying and selling price for the same good in a sense is identified as arbitrage.

Let us look at some standard definitions of arbitrage.

Investopedia defines arbitrage as the simultaneous purchase and sale of an asset in order to profit from the difference in price. Essentially, arbitrage seeks to profit by exploiting price differences of identical or different instruments in different markets or in different forms.

Wikipedia defines arbitrage as the practice of taking advantage of a price difference between two or more markets, striking a combination of matching deals that capitalize on the imbalance between the markets, and the profit so gained is the difference between the market prices.

Look at the supermarket example above. Isn't the supermarket guy making money or profiting from the difference in the wholesale price and the price at which he sells?

This is essentially what arbitraging is – when there is an opportunity to buy at a low price and sell at a high price.

From an academic perspective, in economics and finance, arbitrage is a transaction that is risk free, after deducting transaction costs. Arbitraging works well when both purchasing price and transaction costs are low. Else, one cannot arbitrage.

People who engage in arbitraging are called 'arbitrageurs.' Most arbitrageurs are banks and financial institutions, who generally focus on financial instruments and seek to maximize profit through arbitraging.

While arbitraging on financial instruments is most widely prevalent, a new breed of *neohustlers* have found that there is more to arbitraging than investing only in financial instruments.

Mind the word investment because in the case of financial instruments there is an investment involved, i.e. purchase of shares or bonds or other instruments. One should also wait for the price to appreciate or fluctuate in a day and then sell when the going seems good.

What if I told you that you too can become another neohustler, albeit without making any investment?

Are you agape? I can see your mouth wide open... And if you are not, then you are already aware of this concept and it is nothing new to you.

Whatever be the case, I believe without any investment you can generate passive income, and all you need is a good book that will guide you into this field of generating passive income.

This is the guide you should refer to, and the platform that you will be using to gain a foothold on generating passive income is eBay. The process described here is called eBay Arbitrage.

Let us quickly define what is eBay Arbitrage before getting into the details of this guide.

eBay Arbitrage is purchasing a particular item at a lower price from an online wholesaler and selling it at a higher price on eBay, and pocketing the difference. The key point you need to note here is that you do not physically purchase the item from the wholesaler but list the particular item on your seller account and when the customer places the order on eBay account, you, in turn, place the order from Amazon on the customer's behalf. In essence, Amazon ships the item on your behalf to the customer.

Are you surprised at how this works? Well, that's what I am going to explain in this guide – the how's, do's and don'ts of making money through eBay Arbitrage and clarify any specific questions that you may have. A case study will help you reinforce the concept, before wrapping up with some FAQs and the freedom that you will get by engaging your time on this.

Chapter 1 – Creating an eBay Seller Account

I believe that you are now ready to take up your first step to using eBay to generate passive income. Before you embark on this journey, make sure you can spare about two to four hours a day, spending your time on this activity. There is a specific reason why I am raising this issue, and I will return to this point again, towards the end of this book. Additionally, make sure that you have a fast Internet connection so that the time you spend on Internet is spent worthwhile. A slow internet connection would not give you the benefits that you are seeking.

So, let's embark on this exciting journey to make money through eBay Arbitrage.

Your first task, of course, is to create an eBay Seller Account. Log into www.ebay.com. Depending on your country's residence, you may be directed to the specific country eBay webpage. If www.ebay.com is the only site that you can access in your country, you will have to visit this website.

If you do not have an eBay account, create an eBay account before proceeding to create your seller account.

I have indicated a screenshot to indicate where to create the Seller Account.

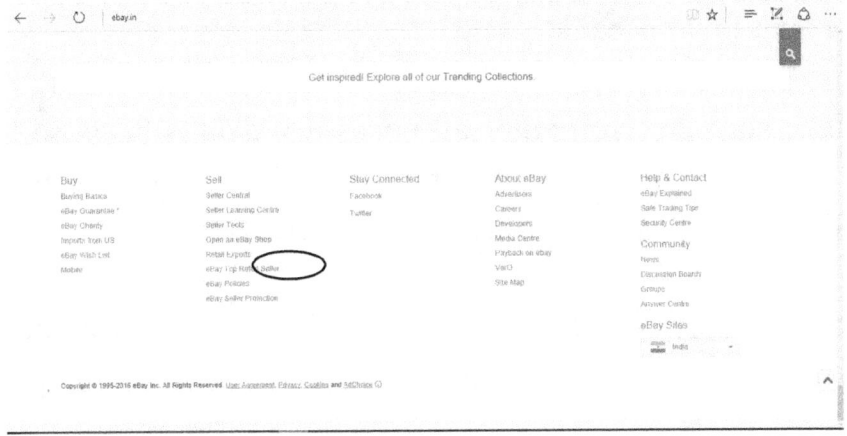

For you to sell items on eBay, you need to have a seller account. A normal account on eBay will only allow you to purchase items as a customer. You cannot be a seller. To be a seller, you will need to register yourself as a seller. Your eBay account allows you to register yourself as a seller. You will need to add appropriate information to ensure that you can be a registered seller.

One of the key things that you will need to remember is that you will need to create a PayPal account so that you can buy and sell items on eBay. If you do not have a PayPal account, you will be prompted to open a PayPal account.

Make sure you enter your bank details, details of your credit cards and debit cards, or any other financial information that you think is relevant to be entered into the PayPal account.

This step is important because all your financial transactions ultimately go to your bank account, for PayPal transfers the amount that you receive to your PayPal account to your bank.

Make sure that you enter all necessary details because the profits that you accrue will be transferred to your bank on a daily / weekly basis based on your preference.

So, with this, you have completed the process of creating the account at eBay and PayPal.

If you are in India, you will specifically have to create a PaisaPay account so that your accrued profits are transferred to your bank account. This is only specific to sellers from India and not rest of the world.

Finally, if you are seeking to sell items internationally, make sure that you have signed up for global shipping program too. Global shipping program allows you to ship your products to international location across the world using eBay's Power Ship Global.

Power Ship Global is a single window shipment solution that is supported by reputed Logistics Service Providers. When you list down your products for selling to international customers, eBay allows you to choose Power Ship Global and avail the logistics and shipping solutions provided by Logistic Services Providers. All you have to do is to select the appropriate logistic service provider from the list that eBay suggests. Remember, as a seller, you are responsible for packing, shipping and delivering the products to the buyers in association with the selected logistic service providers.

Chapter 2 – Finding Products to List

You have now created an eBay account, registered yourself as a seller and linked your PayPal account to your eBay account. I also believe that you have registered yourself for international shipping by signing up for eBay Power Ship Global.

What is your next task? You have the following options:

1. You have products lying with you, i.e. you have physical inventory of products with you and you will have to list them
2. You have to buy your products and build an inventory, and then list them in your seller site
3. Forget about having a physical inventory, and get to online wholesalers to list your products.

The third option is what you need to choose for you are seeking to generate profit without a physical inventory (which in turn, indicates that you have no initial investments).

Let us look at a few online wholesalers from where you can list your products.

Amazon

Amazon is one of the most popular online wholesalers where you can get items at a low rate. You will have to create an account with Amazon so that you can add your items to your shopping cart. You need not purchase the items because when you purchase them Amazon will have to ship the item to you.

You can visit www.amazon.com and search for cheap products with free shipping, as given in the screenshot given below. I have used the search key, "cheap products with free shipping" and the result that emerged is shown in the screenshot.

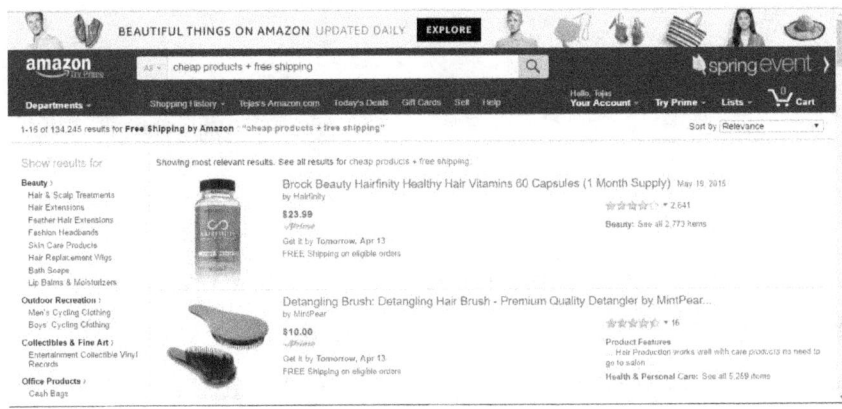

You can search for products for your listing in this manner on eBay.

Home Depot

Another site from where you can get cheap items with free shipping is Home Depot. Home Depot, as the name suggests, specializes in household items, home cleaning products and the like. You can search and filter the ones that you want so that you can add them to your shopping cart.

The screenshot below identifies some products that are cheap and can be shipped for free.

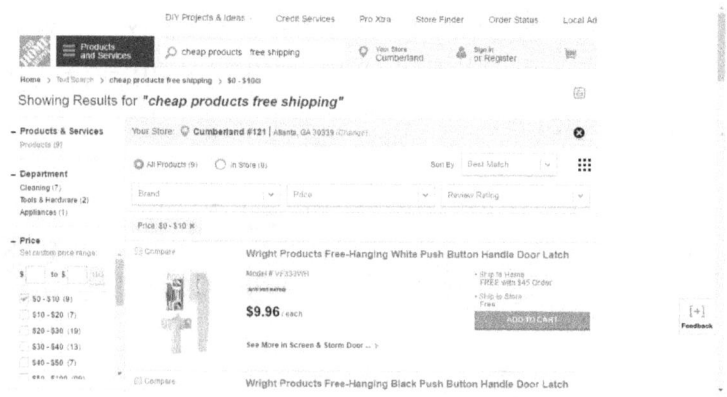

You can find that I have searched for cheap products + free shipping and filtered products that are between $0 - $10. You can add additional filters, based on your preferences.

Wal-Mart

Probably the most famous and recognizable wholesaler is Wal-Mart. I have included a screenshot of Wal-Mart for your reference. I have clicked on Daily Savings Centre so that the cheapest product for the day is reflected on the screen.

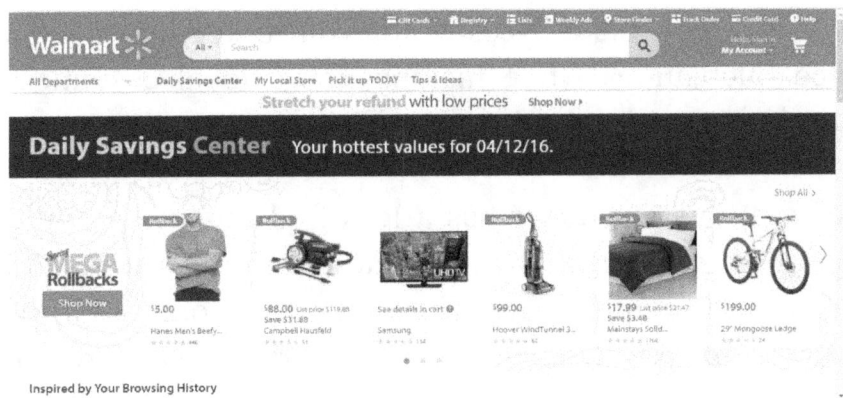

You can follow this strategy to figure out the cheapest product for the day, and add those items to your shopping cart.

You can find numerous such online wholesales which can provide you with cheap products. You need to make sure that you are tuned into the website on a daily or hourly basis so that you are able to determine the actual price.

On the web, price fluctuations are way too common. For example, if the bicycle on the Wal-Mart store is listed at $199.00, it may definitely be possible that the price may either fall or rise. If it falls, you make a profit, while if the price rises, then you may have to bear a loss.

So, a key thing that you need to note here is that when you find the price of a particular item rising one on any of these sites, it is better for you to remove the product from your shopping cart. Else, retain them.

You can use as many sites as you like, but one or two sites for creating the listing can have benefits as well. One or two sites will make it easier for you to keep track of the price fluctuations while making you a loyal customer to that site.

Being a loyal customer has a lot of advantages – you get additional discounts when the site finds that you purchase items on a regular basis. These discounts only add up to your profit. Another site to use to bring loyalty rewards through linking is http://www.ebates.com. This can make your products that your selling anyway though sites, like amazon give you automatic returns for selling through them, and onto eBay. It is a good idea to use as your business grows so you can have a higher margin in your pocket at the end of the day.

If you have an account with a company like Wal-Mart, you have the added advantage of obtaining a credit card that offers a percentage back to you on your purchases. Make sure that you are making a profit on an item that is purchased using the credit card. Else, you may have to bear the credit card bills separately.

With the Wal-Mart credit card, you can use the credit card arbitrage very prudently. When you purchase at Wal-Mart at a low cost, keep the receipt with you and then list the item on eBay at 40% margin. If you bought an item at $10 from Wal-Mart using your credit card, you list the item on eBay at $14.99. This allows you to make enough money but in case there are no buyers for your items, you can return the item back to Wal-Mart within the stipulated time so that you are able to reverse the payment on your credit card.

There's a final word of warning that you need to be aware of. This is with specific reference to Amazon. Amazon offers a service Amazon Prime, a paid membership program that allows customers access to streaming video, music, e-books, free shipping, and a variety of other Amazon services and deals. Amazon Prime costs $99 per annum with a 30-day free trial. All members of Amazon Prime are eligible for one or two-day free shipping on most items, among several other perks.

If you happen to be a member of Amazon Prime and are very active on both Amazon and eBay to ship items to multiple addresses, Amazon Prime may hit an alarm in the system and you may not be able to continue using your Prime account. However, you can use Amazon's standard 3+ day free shipping service so that you do not get into any trouble with Amazon Prime.

Chapter 3 – Listing Your Products

How's it going till now? Got a hang of what to do with the initial round of research on companies like Wal-Mart, Amazon and Home Depot? I believe you did because you would actually be browsing for the details that I have mentioned above. Having said this, your research will not help you in anyway unless you start listing your products on eBay.

Mind you, there are a number of others like you out there who are making money through eBay Arbitrage. They would also be listing their products using the same websites that you would be considering. So, your first question is, with so many competitors out there on eBay, will I be able to make money and profit from the price arbitrage between different sites?

It all boils down to identifying the market. You can scan the websites for various products and check out the ones that your locality may not have, or you believe that your friends and relatives may require. For example, if you find that Home Depot has excellent home cleaning products that are not available in your locality or city, and you are in a different country, say in Africa or Asia, then you will find that this is an excellent opportunity for you to create a market for this product by listing it in your eBay site. So you should go ahead and list it.

The point I am trying to make here is that think of the eBay Arbitrage as a stand-alone business, not as a side business that you would get involved in after office-hours. Just as an entrepreneur would do his market survey on what products or services he/she needs to offer, you need to figure out what products need to be listed and displayed on your eBay seller's page so that you can attract the attention of customers.

In the previous chapter, I had included some screenshots of websites with the search keywords "cheap products + free shipping." You found that there were a number of options that you could choose from. Based on your market survey, you have to identify the products that you want to list on your seller page.

Once you have identified the product / products, mark the product on your seller's page. Ensure that your marked-up price is about 40% more than the price listed on the original website. This is to say that if a product you have chosen to list on your seller page costs $10, the price on your seller page should be at least $14. If you do this, you are well on course to make money through the arbitrage.

Remember, the product you listed may or may not sell, and that depends upon how many people visit your seller's page or the items you have listed in your page.

Once you have identified the product or products to sell, you will need to create a listing. eBay has its own tutorial that you can access to create a listing. Alternatively, you can do your own search to create a listing.

To create your own listing, you can use http://www.title-builder.com/title-builder#. You can find an example in the screenshot below "Canon Powershot s100."

The title builder is a tool that allows you to use it for SEO to optimize your eBay search results. This means that when someone searches for a particular product your results will be displayed first, be it for a limited duration listing or listing for your store.

In order for your product to be displayed at the top of relevant search criteria, this tool will help you with using the exact words that will help you reach the top. All you have to do is to follow the instructions that the tool gives you, and you will find that when a customer searches for an item in your listing, your name will pop at the top, really top.

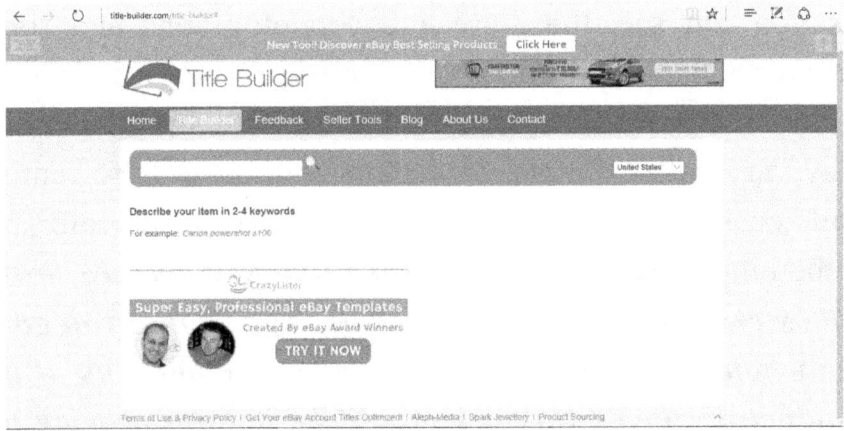

When you search for "Canon Powershot s100," you get some photos and a description. Use a photo that is at least 500px and the description that comes alongside in your listing.

Consider the screenshot that I have taken with the above search criteria.

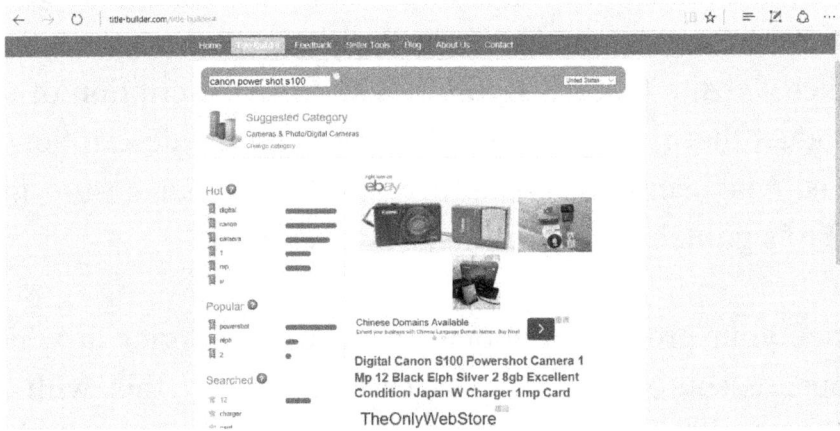

As you can see, there are a few photographs and some keywords of the product. You can use this as it is in your listing. It is worth mentioning that the actual product color may vary based on various factors. This is only to remind your customer that you may not get the exact color but something close to it. *Make sure that you adhere to the 500px criteria here. I would rather suggest that you go to the wholesaler's website and use the photographs of the product displayed there. You will be able to provide the same product to the customer, and hence, when the customer receives the product, he knows that this was exactly what he had ordered.*

Once you have identified the keywords and the photographs to use, you can get to writing the description.

You go back to the original website where the product is available, e.g. Home Depot or Wal-Mart or Amazon or any other website that suits you. Check for a description of the product that is put up there. Do not copy the description as it is. Make minor tweaks here and there but ensure that eBay's guidelines for selling are adhered to.

Price your product at about 40% above the price at which you are sourcing. I have already described this with an example. The 40% margin allows you to make sufficient profit with a relatively small quantity of products sold. Else, you will have to sell a large quantity of products to make the same amount of profit. Another point to remember, which I reiterate even now is that the price on the original websites are not constant. They keep changing. I remember, when I visit a mall and check out the supermarket department, the employees in the store keep announcing that this particular item has a quick discount because only the last 2 – 3 pieces are available.

If this can take place supermarkets and hypermarkets, the online world offers far too many opportunities to keep tweaking and adjusting the price on an hourly basis. So you need to be very careful regarding the pricing.

The 40% rule is again not sanctum sanctorum. Based on your product, you can decide on the actual margin by visiting this website: http://www.newlifeauctions.com/calc.html.

A screenshot of this webpage is given below for your perusal. You can play around with it so that you can come up with the most desirable Net Profit.

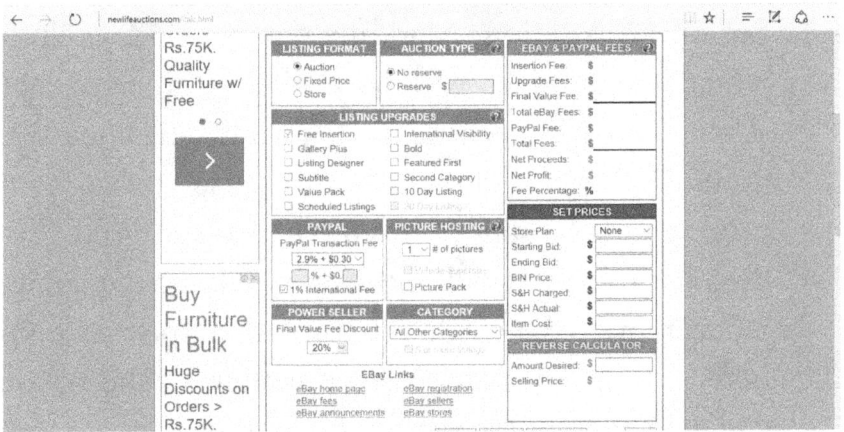

You can select different listing formats to do your calculations like Auction, Fixed Price or Store. Essentially, it is a tool for you to play with. You can check out the price of your item and enter the value in Item Cost. Your BIN Price will be the price at which you plan to sell your product.

I will not go through the various options available to you. I have given you access to this tool. Go ahead, play with it and figure out your best option.

Be sure that if the product that you are planning to list has free shipping, you too include free shipping in your listing. If the product indicates that the shipping is not fee, then do not include free shipping, or vice-versa. As mentioned earlier, in essence, you are transferring the entire look and feel of the product on the original website to your website.

Once you identify the product to be listed, there are two ways in which you can list the products on your eBay seller page.

1. **Set up an Auction:** Mark the number of days during which the product will be available on your store. When you are seeking to take advantage of eBay arbitrage, an auction makes sense because the products that you have listed *may* have a limited time duration during which the item would be available at a cheap price. One rule of thumb that you can follow here is that if the item is on auction in the original site, you can opt for auction in your eBay seller page.

2. **Set up your own store:** The second option is to create your own store, with a number of products that you would like to list on your seller page. In this case, you make an assumption that the price of the goods in the original store will be fairly standardized and will not fluctuate greatly. If this is the case, then it is better for you to list the product in your store. However, having said this, you can also look to sell your goods on auction so that you create an urgency among your customers so that they are compelled to purchase your product.

If you check the screenshot above, you have three options – Auction, Fixed Price and Store in the listing format. You can then decide on what is best for you. With a store, you can set up both an auction or sell the goods at a fixed price. The permutations and combinations are immense, and you only need to know how to play with them. The more adept you become in playing with these permutations and combinations, the better you will be in making money through eBay Arbitrage.

An auction is a good starting point for you. Once you start getting a steady stream of followers, you can hold the items in your listing till they are cancelled.

When you reach a stage where you are ready to create a store, list your products to the maximum number of listings that you can put, or to the maximum amount available to you. For example, if you have a Wal-Mart credit card, you need to have the maximum number of listings based on the amount that you are entitled to using the credit card.

As long as you are signed up for free global shipping, the item is first shipped to eBay's warehouse and then shipped overseas. If the item does not sell, relist the item or change the keywords so that you are able to attract more customers.

I reiterate a point that has been often pointed out earlier too. You are not physically purchasing the item from the original website. When you add an item to your shopping cart in the original website, you will ensure that you add as many items as possible until you reach the limit on your credit card.

For example, if your credit limit on your credit card is $5000, and you have no items in your listing, then you can go ahead and create a listing to the tune of $5000. While it is theoretically possible for you to create a listing more than $5000, it is also possible that all the products that you listed get sold on your page. In this case, you will need to purchase the items from the original site (Wal-Mart), and you will be limited by your credit card's upper limit, and thus, you will end up failing to fulfill some of your customers' orders.

Thus, it always pays to play safe. And in essence, you need ensure that you are well within the available credit limit on the original site.

Once the product is bought from your seller's page, you need to go back to the original site (Wal-Mart, Amazon, Home Depot) and purchase the amount after the amount is credited to your account. List the address of the person who bought the item from your page and include the tracking number too. This will inform the shipper to ship the item directly to the customer. In the process, you have made a direct profit on the product after deducting any transaction costs incurred.

Chapter 4 – Expand Your Service

Congratulations!!! You have made your first sale. Keep it up. So, what are you going to do next? Sit back and enjoy the profit you have made, and then get back to repeating this process?

If you think your duty ends here with the sale, you are terribly mistaken. Recall what I said. Look at this as your standalone business, not as something you do once in a while.

As a businessman, you take care of your customers and vendors **and other service providers**, email them to check if they are satisfied with the services you have provided or take time to give feedback to your vendors. You need to do a similar task here, at least for the next three to four months, especially when you are new to this field.

When you start off your arbitrage business on eBay, you will have a low limit because you need to establish your business. Once your business starts growing, you will need to increase the limit on your listing.

When I did a course on entrepreneurship, I visited a coffee shop to understand how the coffee shop functions, what is the ambience of the place, the number of customers who visit per hour, and the kind of products they sell to their customers. Later, I made an assessment to find out what could be the possible investment for the area, and how the owner / franchise would have started operations.

I had a brief chat with one of the employees at the coffee shop, and figured out that they started with limited products and cash reserves in hand for the next three months, and then expanded to include a number of other products on their menu.

Everywhere, people do not start with too many things on their plate. You start with a limited number of listings, and then you will have to start growing your listing.

In order to do this, for the first few months, at least the first three to four months, it is important that you create a strong working relationship with eBay. Call their helpline to check out your performance. Give them feedback that you are having a great experience selling products on eBay. Understand what your current limits are, and keep seeking avenues to expand your limits.

Do not attempt to ask for a raise in limit the very first time you talk to them. Ask them if there are any other and better ways to list products. eBay organizes webinars every week to help you understand numerous issues. The first three to four months will be a learning exercise and you can take advantage of the webinars that eBay organizes to understand more about the way you can manage your listings.
As a thumb rule, start with one or two products, build a customer base and then move on to adding more products in your listing.

With eBay arbitrage, while you are the customer of the online wholesaler, you have customers too, who buy from you.

Hence, give due importance to them too. Your customers leave you feedback, and may have a number of queries regarding the products that you sell or the service you provide. Some customers may be rude, while others may be polite. Still, others may have a very indifferent attitude. You can gauge this from the feedback that they give you.

Take time off to respond to their feedback. I know it is not possible for you to comment on the feedback that each and every customer gives you. Hence, allocate an hour or so to reply to their comments. It could range from a simple "Thank You" to an elaborate reply to a very nasty criticism.

Let me tell you a story here. It actually drives home a very important point on customer satisfaction. This happened with Home Depot and has become a classical case and anecdote in teaching customer relationship management.

On a hot afternoon, a middle aged lady came into a Home Depot store and said, "I need to replace this set of tires of my car. I have a receipt to show that I bought it here." The employee of the store was flabbergasted, and did not know how to react. He tried to reason with the lady that it was Home Depot, and they don't deal with tires.

But the lady was adamant. She insisted that she gets a replacement for the tire, and did not budge from her place. The employee called the manager of the store. When the manager spoke to the lady, the lady said, "The note outside your store says you replace anything. So, why don't you replace the tires?"

The manager calmed the lady down, walked across the road to the tire showroom, bought a pair of tires for her, and handed it over to her. He even ensured that the showroom guy installed the tire to the wheel. He personally paid the showroom for the car tires and gave the receipt to the lady and sent her off. The lady went off happily.

Later in the day, he hung the tires outside the store with a note, "Satisfied a customer today."

This, my friend, is customer satisfaction. Well, not everyone will be the middle-aged lady, as in Home Depot. The people who buy from you are your genuine customers because they have placed an order on your eBay seller's page.

Hence, it is critical that you have a one-to-one relationship with them. The more you interact with them, the more you make them feel part of your online set up. The next time they come to eBay, they will first check out your store before proceeding to other stores because they know that you will give them valuable time.

This also brings to focus the importance of understanding customer behavior on online retail firms. The online purchasing behavior is very different, and people seek to buy a number of items on impulse. I have bought a number of items on various platforms but I purchase them only when I require them. Whereas, many people buy because there is a massive discount.

There are online stores like Flipkart that offer "Big Billion Day Sale" when prices of many products are extremely low. Well, the concept of low is debatable because it never remains low for more than 5 minutes from the beginning of the sale. Once the sale starts, items are sold like hot cakes, and within no time more than 10,000 different items are sold, and the price jumps to its standard or fair price.

The above example of the "Big Billion Day Sale" is to highlight the importance of understanding online consumer behavior and this will affect the way your page will perform.

Over time, you will learn to create a strong working relationship with both the online wholesalers and customers that will help you to grow your business on eBay.

Chapter 5 – Manage Your Business Through Outsourcing

You are really doing great. You have an excellent "fan" following on eBay, and you are really profiting from your online store. You have been spending a lot of time on eBay and seen your store grow from scratch.

But now, it is time for you to expand not from a customer perspective but from a people perspective. How does people figure in here?

The idea is that you need not to spend a lot of time on doing the listing and taking care of minute things yourself. You have now reached a stage where you need someone to take care of your online store while you can figure out what to do next like open a new store, or go traveling while your store keeps generating profit for you.

But how do you get a person to take care of your store? Let me make this clear here. You are not having a physical store where you need people who can handle customers. While you want someone to handle your online store on your behalf, you need to ensure that they are good enough to communicate with your customers on a regular basis.

The person you need now is a "Professional" lister. A lister is a person who searches various online wholesales and lists the products on your behalf, based on your briefing. He or she is regularly in touch with you regarding the products to list, has extensive discussions with online wholesalers and customers, giving and receiving feedback on your behalf and managing the operations of your online store.

If you recall, I had mentioned that start with only one or two online wholesalers so that you are not too burdened with dealing with too many wholesalers. With a lister, you can add two more vendors, and have the lister manage the relationship with these wholesalers. Or you can hire two listers so that you can expand your store, with products from different wholesalers.

The critical question here is where do you get a lister from?

Check out freelancing platforms like UpWork or Freelancer.com to hire part time or full time listers. You can pay them by the hour or on a lump-sum basis. As a recruiter and manager, you can define the criteria and hire the best possible person for your online store.

If you cannot hire someone from these freelancing platforms, you can try out any outsourced service provider. Make sure that you sign a clearly defined contract with the provider, including the way you will pay the person, and the number of hours he / she needs to put into your online store. Similarly, ensure that the provider invoices you correctly.

Many of the issues pointed out above are taken care of if you are able to hire a lister from the freelancing platforms.

Once you sign up a lister to handle your store, you need to be available for discussions for at least a month. Make sure that you are available for discussions an hour every day. You can ask the lister for a status report on what he has done, what issues he has faced, whether any new products have been listed, what is the sale for the day and many other more. At the same time, make sure that you have at least $5000 credit limit so that your lister is able to work without any hindrances.

While you will get a mail on the sale of the products on your store, it is important for you to keep in touch with your lister regularly, and ensure that your online store never sleeps.

Chapter 6 – Tim, the Online Store Expert

Before I wind up this guide, let me share a small story of Tim, who used eBay Arbitrage to generate passive income.

Tim has a store on eBay and has been browsing for products to list on his store. He finds a lovely pair of socks on Amazon and decides to sell and list this item on his store. He likes this because there is a craze for wearing designer socks in his city and he has a clientele of women who are his regular customers. His online store has been quite famous for the designer ladies' clothes that he sells online, and his reputation as an online store owner is excellent.

He decides to list this item on his website. He takes a screenshot of the product or clicks on the images and saves them on his computer. He takes the description of the product and copies to a word document that he will use later. He also uses appropriate tools to find keywords and titles that match SEO requirements.

Once he has completed these tasks, he goes back to the description that he downloaded from Amazon, tweaks and edits them to suit his requirements.

The price on Amazon is $10, and offers a free 3-day shipping. He includes this in his description, but with a catch. He knows that he has to pay some fees to eBay and probably to PayPal too. Since shipping is free, he has no shipping costs. After some calculations, he finds that the best price he can quote is $14.99.

He is now ready to make the listing go live. He lists the product on his store, with the images he got from Amazon, and the description he edited. The listing goes live, and is live for three days.

He sits back, waiting for his customers to purchase the product while he gets ready to list more products till his listing is full.

Now, put yourself in Tim's place and enjoy the freedom that Tim is enjoying.

Freedom: Your Ultimate Gain

I used an important word in the last line of the previous chapter. You guessed it right, "Freedom." What does freedom mean to you?

Freedom would mean a lot of things for a lot of people. For me, freedom here would mean freedom from a straitjacketed, 9-5 job. Your online store is open 24 hours a day, 365 days a year. So you are literally earning money right from the moment you open your store till the day "You" decide to close it down. But passive income is so addictive, once you start, you will never want to give up.

Start slow at first, spend about an hour to about four hours a day. In fact, the more time you spend in the beginning, the more you will start making, till you reach your saturation point.

You can outsource the work to a lister, and handle your store from a management perspective, taking a sneak-peek once or twice a day to ensure that your store is on track. If you get an excellent lister who can duplicate your tasks and manage it independently, you are free to do whatever you want.

You had plans to go on a foreign trip, through Asia and the Orient? Or wanted to write a book that has been eating dust for the past several years? Or you want to learn a new hobby? Whatever your plans are, they are all yours to take, and even when you are on vacation, your store will never sleep for you.

For more from this author please visit:

twk-publishing.com

www.ingramcontent.com/pod-product-compliance
Lightning Source LLC
Chambersburg PA
CBHW070418190526
45169CB00003B/1316